— Animal Trackers —
SAVING ANIMAL
SPECIES

Tom Jackson

raintree
a Capstone company — publishers for children

Raintree is an imprint of Capstone Global Library Limited, a company incorporated in
England and Wales having its registered office at 7 Pilgrim Street, London EC4V 6LB
Registered company number 6695582

www.raintree.co.uk
myorders@raintree.co.uk

ISBN: 978-1-4747-0236-2

For Brown Bear Books Ltd:
Text: Tom Jackson
Designer: Lynne Lennon
Design Manager: Keith Davis
Editorial Director: Lindsey Lowe
Children's Publisher: Anne O'Daly
Picture Manager: Sophie Mortimer
Production Director: Alastair Gourlay

British Library Cataloguing in Publication Data
A full catalogue record for this book is available from the British Library.

Acknowledgements
t=top, c=centre, b=bottom, l=left, r=right

Front cover: Pete Oxford/Minden/FLPA
1, Vadim Petrakov/Shutterstock; 4, Sombra/Shutterstock; 5tl, Vladimir Sevrinovsky/Shutterstock; 5tr, Dorling Kindersley/
Thinkstock; 6, Rich Carey /Shutterstock; 7, Ethan Daniels/Shutterstock; 8, Janelle Lugge/Shutterstock; 9t, Sura Nualpradid/
Shutterstock; 9b, Dean Bertoncelj/Shutterstock; 10, Vadim Petrakov/Shutterstock; 11, Harald Toepfer/Shutterstock; 12c, Mike
Lane/iStock/Thinkstock; 12b, Vitali Hulai/iStock/Thinkstock; 13t, Farbled/Shutterstock; 14, Marco Rubino/Shutterstock; 15,
RGB Ventures/Superstock/Alamy; 16, FLPA/Alamy; 17t, Pete Niessen/Shutterstock; 17b, Michael Zysman /Shutterstock; 18,
Steve Mart/Shutterstock; 19cl, John Moore/Getty Images News/Thinkstock; 19tr, Tom Dowd/Dreamstime; 20, Susan Adams/
Shutterstock; 21, AFP/Getty Images; 22, Andrew Harrington/Nature PL; 23t, Eric Gevaert/Shutterstock; 23b, Jorge Sierra/
Biosphoto/FLPA; 24, Feather Collector/Shutterstock; 25t, Anneka/Shutterstock; 25c, Sergey Krasnoshchokov /Shutterstock; 26,
Creative Nature/Shutterstock; 27t, David Hilcher/Shutterstock; 27b, Blue Orange Studio/Shutterstock; 28, Xavier Vila/Alamy; 29t,
Iurii/Shutterstock; 29b, Natural History Museum/Alamy.

All Artworks © Brown Bear Books Ltd
Brown Bear Books has made every attempt to contact the copyright holder.
If anyone has any information please contact licensing@brownbearbooks.co.uk.

Some words are shown in bold, **like this**. You can find out
what they mean by looking at the glossary.

Printed in China
19 18 17 16 15
10 9 8 7 6 5 4 3 2 1

CONTENTS

WHY WE SAVE ANIMAL SPECIES

Many animals are **endangered**. They include a quarter of the world's **mammals** and nearly half of all frog **species**, as well as many other types of animals. These species need to be protected by humans or they will become **extinct**.

An axolotl is an endangered salamander that lives in Mexico. The species is very rare and is found in only two lakes.

CONSERVATION

The process of saving animal species is called conservation. Conservationists use science to figure out which species need protecting. A list of endangered species is organised by the International Union for Conservation of Nature (IUCN) based in Switzerland. The list has 76,000 animals in need of protection.

This saiga is living in a zoo. There are only a few thousand left in the wild. These Asian animals need protecting because people hunt them for their unusual horns.

UNDERSTANDING THREATS

Before conservationists can protect a species, they have to work out what is making it endangered. Scientists track endangered animals to see where they go and how they behave. That helps them to find out what kinds of threats the species faces. Different animals are affected in different ways by the same problem. The biggest threats are damage to **habitats**, hunting by people and **pollution**.

SAVING SPECIES

Conservationists protect habitats to ensure that endangered species have a place to live. They also breed animals in captivity and reintroduce them to the wild. In other cases, conservationists use technology to give the endangered animals a helping hand.

The dodo, from the island of Mauritius in the Indian Ocean, became extinct in the 1600s. They were hunted by sailors who visited the island. This is an example of how human activities can wipe out a species forever.

FACT: No Yangtze River dolphins have been seen since 2002. Scientists believe this species may be extinct.

HABITAT DECLINE

Habitat destruction is the biggest threat to animals. A few animals can live in many habitats, but most species can survive only in one place. Conservationists work to protect those places and ensure the survival of threatened species.

SPECIALIST SPECIES

A few animals, such as rats and mice, are generalists. This means that they can survive in many different types of habitat, from sewers to jungles. However, most species are specialists. This means they have a particular way of life and live in a particular habitat.

A digger is clearing a patch of rainforest in Borneo. The land is being turned into a plantation to grow palm trees, which produce oil used in food.

A giant panda is a specialist. It eats bamboo in mountain forests in China. If those forest habitats are cut down, the panda cannot just go and live somewhere else. Pandas and many other endangered species are threatened because their special habitats are being destroyed.

HUMAN ACTIVITY

Habitats are damaged or destroyed by different types of human activity. People cut down forests to make way for farms and mines. They use the trees for firewood and for making buildings. Wetlands are areas of land that are covered in shallow water for long periods. People drain them so they can use them as fields or for building homes.

All of these activities – farming, building houses and finding fuel – are very important for humans. However, these activities threaten many species. Conservationists try to balance the needs of people with protecting the habitats that animals need to survive.

Coral reefs are dying because the water around them has too much **carbon dioxide** mixed into it. The carbon dioxide comes from humans burning fuels to power cars and produce electricity.

PLANTING FORESTS

Forests have more species living in them than any other habitat on land. One of the main jobs of conservationists is planting new forests where old ones have been cleared away.

Saplings planted in a forest clearing have plastic guards around them. The guards protect the young trees from plant-eating animals and help them to grow straight up.

ANCIENT HABITAT

It takes a very long time for a forest to grow. The large trees in a forest may be more than 100 years old. Forest soil has to have nutrients for the trees and all the other plants. These chemicals come from the rotting remains of dead plants and animals. It takes **decades** for the soil to develop the right mix of nutrients for all the forest plants.

REPLANTING TREES

An ancient forest can be cut down in a few days. The logs and branches may be burned to clear them away quickly. Most of the animals that lived in the forest will eventually die without their habitat.

Conservationists work to stop too much forest from being cut down. They also **restore** areas of forest that have been damaged or cleared. Conservationists grow many types of saplings in plant nurseries. Then they replant these young trees along with other forest plants. Within a few years, the new plants will fill the gap in the habitat.

Conservationists use catapults to fire tree seeds into a replanted **mangrove** forest. This ensures new plants keep growing as the swampy habitat develops.

TECHNOLOGY: Bat boxes

When replanting tropical forests, conservationists put up roosting boxes for fruit bats. The large bats are very good at **dispersing** the seeds of fruit trees. The bats pick the fruits and fly off to eat them. The bats then drop the seeds in another part of the forest.

SAVING WETLANDS

Wetlands are areas like swamps and marshes where the land is covered in shallow **fresh water** for at least part of the year. These places are important habitats for many species, such as frogs and birds. Many wetlands need protecting.

LUSH LAND

Wetlands have a high **biodiversity.** They are filled with many unusual species, such as fish and frogs, that bury themselves in mud when the water dries out in summer. The animals stay underground until the land is flooded again after heavy rains.

The capybara is a wetland animal from South America. It is the world's largest rodent. The capybara is the size of a sheep but is related to mice and rats.

A fishing boat that once sailed on the Aral Sea is now stuck on dry land.

WOW!

The Aral Sea in Central Asia was once the fourth largest lake in the world. Today most of it is a desert, and the rest has split into several much smaller lakes. The sea's water came from the Amu River, which starts in Afghanistan. That water is now diverted to irrigate farms upstream. None of it reaches the Aral Sea any more.

Many **migrating** birds visit wetlands as they make their long journeys. The wetlands provide the birds with food, such as water plants and bugs, while the birds take a rest.

THREATS TO WETLANDS

Large amounts of water make wetlands very fertile places. That is why many of them are drained to make way for fields. However, scientists have discovered that draining wetlands is very bad for the **environment.** As well as being important places for many endangered species, these habitats prevent flooding during storms. The swamp areas absorb the water that would otherwise rush further inland.

Wetlands are often located beside the ocean, river mouths or near large lakes. Many wetlands are being covered over to make shipping ports and holiday resorts. Conservationists work with construction workers to make sure things can be built without destroying all of the valuable habitat.

Freshwater habitats

Natural ponds and marshes are under threat from human activity. However, it is possible to rebuild these small, but important, habitats.

Even a small woodland pool or patch of marshland in a meadow can be home to dozens of unusual animal species. These kinds of freshwater habitats can be recreated in gardens and parks.

Life in water

Freshwater pools and slow-flowing rivers are important habitats for **amphibians** and insects. Amphibians include animals such as frogs and newts. Most of them need a supply of water to survive. Frogs start life as tadpoles, which swim in water. The adults can come onto land but need to keep damp at all times.

Many insects, including dragonflies, have to lay their eggs in water. When the eggs hatch, the young, or larvae (right), live underwater and only fly in the air as adults.

Crested newt

The crested newt (above) is endangered in Great Britain. Before any construction takes place near a freshwater habitat, conservationists must check if the rare newt is living there. If newts are found, they must be moved to a new habitat.

New habitat

Natural freshwater habitats are often drained during construction and by farmers. But they can be rebuilt somewhere else. Even a garden pond can be an excellent freshwater habitat if it is built in the correct way. The habitat needs deep areas filled with plants and shallow parts where the ground is waterlogged. Animals will find the new pond and set up home.

The salmon ladder has many small steps for fish to jump up.

WOW!

Salmon swim upriver to breed. The powerful fish swim against the current and leap over waterfalls to get upstream. But salmon cannot jump over a dam that is built across a river. Conservationists build salmon ladders around dams. The ladder is an artificial channel for the salmon to follow up and over the high dam.

The deep section does not freeze in winter. It is where newts and fish survive during cold periods.

Pond habitat

A pond can be made from a simple hole dug in the ground. The hole is lined with a plastic sheet covered in soil, which stops the water from draining away. Adding rocks and logs creates more places for plants to grow and for animals to hide.

Small trees and bushes grow on the banks.

The shallow sections make it easier for animals to climb into and out of the water.

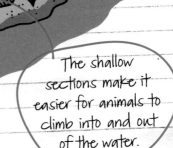

GREEN ROOFS

A city is not a natural habitat. There is not much room for animals to live. However, new conservation ideas are creating habitats in cities. They include turning roofs, bridges and even old railways into wildlife gardens.

CITY ANIMALS

The city is home to many animals. Most are generalists that can find food in a wide range of places. City animals include rats, pigeons, squirrels, foxes and even some types of deer. People think these species are **pests.** The animals eat rubbish, dig up gardens and damage trees. Conservationists try to get non-pest species to live in cities. They do this by converting unused areas of a city into wildlife habitats.

This wildlife park is planted on an old railway line that runs through New York City. It provides habitats for butterflies and birds in the heart of the huge city.

This osprey has built a nest next to the spacecraft **hangar** at the Kennedy Space Center in Florida.

UNUSED SPACES

Cities are crowded places. Buildings and roads cover almost all the space. However, there are some empty, unused spaces where a wildlife habitat can be set up. The most common unused spaces are the flat roofs of buildings. These can be covered with soil and turned into gardens, with shrubs and trees. There are even little ponds the size of a bucket.

Roof habitats provide homes for songbirds, such as sparrows, which find it hard to build nests in big cities. A roof garden is also good for the building. The layer of soil stops heat from escaping from the roof in winter. It also absorbs the sun's warmth in summer, so the rooms underneath stay cool.

JOIN IN

Build a wildlife refuge

It is possible to build a wildlife refuge just about anywhere in a city. Even a balcony garden or large window box will provide habitats for butterflies and other bugs. Search online for these organisations to find out more about green roofs and city wildlife gardens.

Royal Society for the Protection of Birds (RSPB)
Royal Horticultural Society (RHS)
The Wildlife Trusts

FACT: A garden roof is not a new idea. Tall grass grew on top of Viking houses.

HELPING THREATENED SPECIES

Scientists often discover that a species is threatened because humans stop it from behaving in a natural way. Conservationists study how different animals behave. This helps them to work out how to save each species.

LIFE CYCLE

Every animal has a life cycle. This is a set of stages that the animal goes through as it grows, finds a mate and has **offspring**. Anything that interrupts that life cycle will stop the animal from having offspring. The species will gradually become more rare and may be in danger of becoming extinct.

A toad travels through a tunnel to reach the pool where it breeds. The tunnel was built specially for the toads so they do not have to cross a road.

JOIN IN

checking threats

The IUCN's Red List contains information about every endangered animal species. To explore the different threats affecting species, search online for:

IUCN Red List

FINDING PROBLEMS

Conservationists track the movements and behaviour of endangered animals to work out how to help them. One of the common problems they study using tracking is to do with migration. Migrating animals follow the same routes each year. If the route is blocked, the animals cannot complete their life cycle.

Another threat comes from pet collectors. They take young animals from the wild before they can breed. Pollution can also affect animals' bodies and stop them from producing enough young.

TECHNOLOGY: Turtle lights

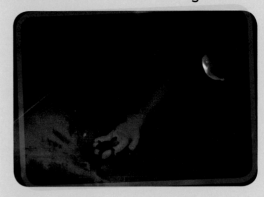

Sea turtles lay their eggs on beaches. When the baby turtles hatch, they use moonlight to find their way to the ocean. Artificial lights confuse the turtles' sense of direction and many never reach the water. Turtles cannot see red light. Using red "turtle-safe" lights on beaches means more young turtles will survive.

A man sells parrots and a lizard taken from the jungle. Collecting pets from the wild is against the law because it endangers many animal species.

Drone patrols

African elephants are threatened by **poachers**. These criminals want the animals' ivory tusks. Armed rangers use **drone** aircraft to watch over the elephant herds.

Elephants live in Africa's forests and grasslands. They walk hundreds of kilometres every week. It is difficult to know where they are all the time. Video from high-flying drones makes it easier to spot herds on the ground and see when they are in danger.

Tusk hunters

Elephants are famous for their long tusks. The tusk is a long tooth. It is made from a hard, white material known as ivory. For centuries ivory was used to make jewellery and other objects. For example, white piano keys were once made from ivory. To get ivory, hunters have to kill elephants. In the 1980s, conservationists realised that too many elephants were being killed. One hundred years ago there were 5 million African elephants. Today there are only 500,000.

In 1990 it was made illegal to hunt for elephants and sell ivory. But poachers are still killing elephants, and the species is still endangered.

Eye in the sky

The drone gives rangers a good view of the ground. It has a powerful video camera that sends pictures back to the ground using radio waves. This is similar to the technology used in mobile phones.

Armed patrols

African elephants are protected by teams of armed park rangers. They are allowed to shoot anyone found poaching ivory. They use drones and other technology to protect the animals in the wild.

Ivory trade

Even though it is against the law, people will pay very high prices for ivory. Heavily armed rangers (left) search for poacher camps (right) where the ivory is stored. The ivory is then burned.

High-tech defences

Elephants are fitted with trackers. These send radio signals that show rangers where the animals are. If poachers are seen near a group of elephants, rangers are sent in to stop them.

1 A drone aircraft takes videos of the ground showing any poachers in the area.

5 Armed rangers are sent to arrest the poachers and protect the animals.

2 Video from the drone is watched by park rangers in a mobile command unit.

4 Tracking device tells rangers where the elephant is.

3 Poacher approaches elephant.

CAPTIVE-BREEDING PROGRAMMES

In some cases the threats to a species are so great that the animals cannot be protected in the wild. Conservationists catch as many animals as possible. They raise them in **captivity**, in places such as zoos.

The scimitar oryx used to live wild in the Sahara Desert. In the 1990s these antelopes became extinct in the wild. Today all of the species live in wildlife parks and zoos.

NEARLY EXTINCT

Conservationists always try to save species by making it safe for them to live in their natural habitats. However, in extreme cases, people have to remove animals from the wild to stop the species from becoming extinct.

TECHNOLOGY: Test-tube pandas

There are hundreds of giant pandas in the world's zoos. However, very few panda cubs have been born in captivity. Conservationists are using in-vitro fertilisation (IVF). In IVF, eggs and sperm are taken from the animals and mixed in a laboratory. Then embryos (known as test-tube babies) are put into a female panda. The cubs (left) grow inside and are born in the normal way.

BREEDING PROGRAMMES

Putting animals in a safe zoo or safari park is not enough to save the species. The captive animals must still breed as they do in the wild. Zookeepers try to make the animals' homes as much like a natural habitat as possible. Large animals, such as rhinoceroses, need a lot of space to walk around. Species that live alone in the wild, such as giant pandas, need to be kept apart until it is time to breed.

Each zoo can have only a few of each endangered species. As a result, the animals in one zoo are often closely related and cannot breed with each other. Conservationists arrange for endangered animals to be transferred to zoos all over the world. This ensures the species stays healthy and strong.

FACT: There are 32 animal species that do not live in the wild and survive only in zoos.

REINTRODUCTION PROGRAMMES

Breeding endangered animals in zoos is only the first step in saving a species. Once there are enough animals, conservationists will return them to the wild using a system called reintroduction.

STAYING WILD

The way animals live in a zoo can be very different from how they live in the wild. They do not need to find food – the zookeepers give them what they need. Zoo animals do not need to build a den or nest, and they never meet other species.

Before a captive-bred animal can be reintroduced to the wild, it needs to learn how to look after itself. Animals need to learn where to find food and make a home. They need to learn how to defend themselves and how to communicate with each other.

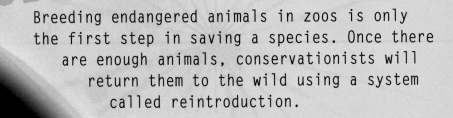

A black-footed ferret is released into the wild in the U.S. state of Montana. Conservationists have already built an underground den for it.

EARLY MISTAKE

Some early reintroduction programmes did not go well. Golden lion tamarins were bred in zoos and then released into a protected area of forest in Brazil. Most of them died, falling from the trees. The monkeys had grown up in zoos where they climbed on fixed logs. The animals were not used to branches that swayed as they ran along them. After that, zoos let the monkeys live in real trees. The reintroduction was a great success from then on.

LIFE SKILLS

Reintroduction is more difficult for animals that have complex **social** systems. When the first zoo-bred giant pandas were released, many were killed in fights with the wild pandas. The zoo pandas did not understand how wild pandas lived in a **territory**. Conservationists now work hard to make sure animals live in captivity in the same way as their wild cousins do.

About 500 golden lion tamarins live in zoos. That is about a seventh of the entire global **population**.

Captive Iberian lynxes are taught how to catch live rabbits. They will be able to catch their own food when they are returned to the wild.

23

Saving sandpipers

Conservationists have saved spoon-billed sandpipers from extinction by moving their eggs halfway across the world.

The spoon-billed sandpiper lives in the marshes of eastern Russia. It is one of the rarest bird species in the world. There are only around 200 adult birds living in the wild.

Extinction threat

The spoon-billed sandpiper lives along the Pacific coast of East Asia. In autumn the birds fly as far south as Vietnam and Myanmar. In spring they fly north to Siberia in Russia. The birds breed and lay eggs in summer. They make small nests in the grass that grows in the marshlands.

The sandpipers have become very rare, very quickly. That is because many of the wetlands where they feed on their long journey have been drained in the last few years. Each year fewer birds make it back to Siberia to breed. If nothing had been done, the species would be extinct by now.

Spoon-shaped bill

The spoon-billed sandpiper is a wading bird. It feeds on bugs that live in shallow marshes. The bird uses its spoon-shaped bill to feel for prey in the muddy water. It walks along swishing its bill from side to side in the water. The bird gobbles up any bug that the bill touches.

Rescue mission

In 2013 a team of English conservationists travelled to a remote part of eastern Siberia (below) to collect spoon-billed sandpiper eggs. The eggs and chicks were taken to England for captive breeding.

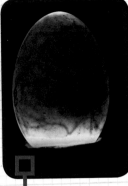

The dark spot is the eye of a chick inside this egg.

After they have collected a sandpiper egg from the nest, the conservationists need to check that there is a chick growing inside. They do this by shining a bright light through the shell. That shows up what is inside. An expert uses the light to see if a chick is growing inside the egg. This method is known as candling.

Long journey

Sandpiper eggs have been taken from nests in Siberia and flown 8,000 kilometres (5,000 miles) to a bird centre in England. The centre specialises in breeding this type of wetland bird. If the bird's habitat in Siberia can be restored, the bird will be reintroduced there.

1 Sandpiper eggs are taken from nests made on the ground in the marshlands of Siberia.

2 Some of the eggs hatch as they are being taken by ship to the airport.

3 The eggs and chicks are flown all the way to England.

4 The young sandpipers are raised in a bird centre. The following year they will have their own chicks.

TACKLING PREDATORS

Most species have natural predators (other animals that hunt them). However, when humans introduce new predators to an area, some species have no defence against them.

IN BALANCE

Most animal species live in just one part of the world. They are part of a community of animals that lives there. Some species in that community are predators that prey on the others. There is a balance between the numbers of predators and prey. If a new predator is added to the community, the balance is lost.

Tuataras are very rare. When European people first moved to New Zealand, where tuataras live, they brought rats with them. The rats ate the tuataras' eggs. The reptiles survive only on tiny islands where there are no rats.

The fence is 1.8 metres (6 feet) tall, which is higher than a dingo can jump.

WOW!

Dingoes are wild dogs that live in Australia. They are a threat to farm animals and some native species, such as the cat-like quolls. To control the number of dingoes, the world's longest fence was built across south-east Australia in 1885. It is 5,614 kilometres (3,488 miles) long. Most dingoes live north of the fence. In this area there are fewer kangaroos and emus than there are to the south. This is because they are hunted by dingoes.

INTRODUCED PREDATORS

Humans have spread many animals around the world. For example, they took horses to America and rabbits to Australia. Predators have also moved with people. They include pet cats, working dogs and pest species such as rats. Many local animal species had no defence against the new predators. As a result, the local animals have become endangered

Once a new predator species has made its home in an area, it is very difficult to get rid of it. It is easier to move the endangered animals to a place where the predator doesn't live. Large fences may be put up to keep the dangerous species out. Rare animals are relocated to islands where the predator cannot go.

Boobies from certain Pacific islands have no natural fear. They have no defence against introduced predators that steal their eggs.

With so many animal species in danger, conservationists will never be able to save every one of them from becoming extinct.

BIG PROBLEM

Some scientists think that as many as 35 species of plant and animal are becoming extinct every day. This is just a guess. It is based on the idea that scientists have described about 1 million living species so far. There are perhaps 10 times as many that people know nothing about. Many of those species will be endangered, but people can do nothing to protect them. It is also possible that endangered species we do know about, such as tigers and gorillas, will be extinct soon unless humans change the way they view nature and wildlife.

A protester dressed as a pig is encouraging governments to make laws that protect animals and their environments.

ANIMAL PRODUCTS

People hunt many endangered animals. Some people think the body parts of some animals make good medicines. This is usually not true. Scientists can prove that these medicines do not work.

BETTER FARMING

People are often unable to protect natural habitats because they need to clear areas of land to grow enough food to eat. To protect habitats in the future, high-tech agricultural techniques will make farming more efficient. This will allow the world's farms to grow enough food for everyone. The technology could include irrigation that saves water and new crops that grow very fast. One day science could make it possible to feed everyone without building new farms and destroying habitats. This is the biggest challenge for scientists in the future.

Future cities may not damage natural habitats as much as they do now.

This is a quagga. It had fewer stripes than other species of zebra.

WOW!

The quagga is a type of zebra that became extinct in 1870. For 30 years a team in South Africa has been trying to breed common zebras back into quaggas. The team uses the methods that pet breeders and farmers use to create new animal breeds. Most scientists say that even if the team succeeds, the new breed will not be a true quagga – just an animal that looks like one.

GLOSSARY

amphibian animal that spends its life in water as well as on land

biodiversity variety of plant and animal species in an area

captivity situation in which an animal is kept under human care and not allowed to return to its natural habitat

carbon dioxide gas released by burning

decade set of ten years

disperse spread out

drone unpiloted aircraft

endangered in danger of becoming extinct

environment surroundings or conditions in which a person, animal or plant lives

extinct no longer existing

freshwater water without salt in it

habitat place where animals or plants live and grow

hangar building for housing aircraft

irrigate supply water to plants

mammal animal with hair that feeds its young on milk

mangrove forest that grows in a swamp

migrating make a regular journey to find food, find mates or raise young

native from the local area

offspring young animal

pest animal that causes a problem for humans

poacher hunter who kills animals that are protected by laws

pollution damage to the environment by something harmful

population group of animals of one species

restore change something back to its original state

sapling young tree

social living in a group

species group of animals that can breed with each other

territory region controlled by an animal. The animal finds all its food in the territory and tries to stop other members of its species from living there.

READ MORE

Emperor Penguin (A Day in the Life: Polar Animals). Katie Marsico. Oxford, UK: Raintree, 2012.

Endangered Animals (Eyewitness). Ben Hoare. London: Dorling Kindersley, 2010.

Endangered Oceans: Investigating Oceans in Crisis (Endangered Earth). Jody Sullivan Rake. North Mankato, Minn.: Capstone Press, 2015.

Sharks (Amazing Animals). Jen Green. London: Hachette Children's Books, 2013.

The 10 Most Endangered Animals (10). Barbara Winter. London: Franklin Watts, 2008.

Tigers (Amazing Animals). Sally Morgan. London: Hachette Children's Books, 2013.

INTERNET SITES

RSPB
Ideas for attracting wildlife to your garden.
www.rspb.org.uk/makeahomeforwildlife/wildlifegarden

Royal Horticultural Society
Gardening for wildlife.
https://www.rhs.org.uk/science/conservation-biodiversity/wildlife

The Wildlife Trusts
Information about the creation of 'living landscapes' to encourage biodiversity.
http://www.wildlifetrusts.org/localwildlifesites

IUCN Red List
A list of the world's endangered animals.
www.iucnredlist.org

INDEX